SET-PA-RATION

*Rising From Loneliness to
Self-Discovered Truths*

Dr. Dana R. Johnson

JATNE Publishing
Sumter, SC

Published by JATNE Publishing August 1, 2025.

ISBN: 978-1-958117-22-4 (paperback)
ISBN: 978-1-958117-25-5 (eBook)

Library of Congress Control Number: 2025905113

This book is dedicated to my daughters,
nieces and goddaughters.

TABLE OF CONTENTS

REVIEWS

"This book is very encouraging and has helped me escape dark places. The anointing in this book will help many to maneuver through troubled times. Such a light for the world!"

– *Jesse Jr*, *Bold Church Youth Minister*

"Dr. Dana has done an excellent job inspiring readers of the importance of self-discovery and relying on God for guidance and strength for transformative results. I felt her sincere empathy for those dealing with loneliness and her desire to see people living free from emotional bondage. Her transparency in sharing her story is like oxygen... I'm ready to rise and breathe new life!"

– *Janice Burton,* *Janice J. Burton Enterprises, The Marriage Planning Mogul, Speaker, Dating Relationship Coach*

"I love Dr. Dana Johnson's spirit. She always amazes me with her inspiration and strength. The message is a light to every reader."

– *Dr. Ingrid Bynum,* *K-12 Educator*

"In this book, Dr. Dana walks us through her powerful journey of self-discovery. We often don't like being alone, but in this book, you will discover things about yourself that God can only reveal in alone times. We often see separation as a negative thing, but we discover in this book that there is a SET purpose even in separation."

– *Prophetess Lekethia Polanco,* Founder, Vessel of Honor Ministries

"Dr. Dana Johnson is an impactful speaker, writer, identity/rise coach. Her latest book reminds us to understand who God says we are and to value our self-worth. She is the right person to inspire such things because I have seen her confidence rise to new heights. I have witnessed Dr. Dana encouraging women to soar above their circumstances just as she did and continues to do—as she trusts in God throughout the work He's doing in her. The bottom is that she will do whatever Dr. Dana wants to do. That's who she is: an inspirational thought leader who continues to do her work within to see what we see on the outside. That is so admirable. Moreover, she gently pushes women to rise and to know their identity with God through self-discovery and a deeper understanding of their purpose and calling.

Dr. Dana Johnson inspires others to do, and although that's not easy, she does it miraculously well. I'm proud of Dr. Dana and how she inspires me and many other women."

– **Sharon Shannon,** *Founder/CEO of Women of Movement*

FOREWORD

I am Apostle Mattie Muse. Writing a foreword for Dr. Dana Johnson is a pleasure and honor. First, I would like to say that she is my niece and I have known her all her life. I am proud of the woman she has become as she serves the Lord. I have watched her walk from one level to another in this journey called life.

In this book, I see a heart seeking to help others. As you read along, I believe you will see what you have been experiencing and receive the answers you have been seeking. You will discover that you are not alone in your journey as she shares hers with wisdom. This book is full of insight, which can help one break free of bondages that have held them spellbound, perhaps for years. It brings to light things you thought no one else would understand.

This book covers much counseling as Dr. Johnson is led by the Spirit of the Lord in every chapter. She shares much of herself and is transparent. I believe young adults should read this book, especially those in relationships who have been in situations they have not overcome, which carried them into their current relationships. I also believe adults should read this to gain insight. Sometimes, adults have endured unsolved traumas, so they carry them into their families. Their families become affected and the traumas travel down through generations.

Dr. Johnson received wisdom through her life's journey from the Lord Jesus Christ. No man or woman can satisfy the things she talks about, only the Lord. Make a space to sit and read slowly to take in the wisdom and knowledge the Lord has given her.

In Christ Alone,
Apostle Mattie Muse
Way of Freedom Ministries

PREFACE

Life experiences, circumstances and struggles are a thread that binds us all. It is a shared journey and, unfortunately, some never fully overcome their pain and hurt. I, too, have faced many trials, challenges and obstacles in my life, some easier to overcome than others. The easiest were the ones that went against my faith, morals and values. The toughest challenges were the ones I was unprepared for, but each difficulty was a steppingstone to help overcome the next.

I am very compassionate when I see others struggling to overcome challenges I went through, refusing to let go of situations that devalue their worth or heading toward disappointment, hurt and pain. I want to share my testimony of how God has brought me out of empty and dark spaces and spiritually positioned me into a place where I breathe out and release emotional strains to live, enjoy life and be content.

The power of thoughts will move or halt anything; the power of a word can break or destroy anything; and the inability to forgive is haunting. Action is in the thought and manifestation is in the mouth. A person can think of everything they want, but it will not manifest until they speak from the mouth of their heart. I have learned to create in my mind and form peace in my heart that no man can understand unless they experience it for themselves. The greatest treasures of life exist where no one wants to be. No one wants to live in a world of loneliness, nevertheless, being alone is where the King exists. It is the space God occupies, waiting to fill it with us, and that is when the sad story becomes a love story.

I write this book for the lonely and everyone struggling to find fulfillment in their void. God is always present. He is like the person who appears when we think we are sitting in a place and we think no one else is there or sees us, and then we notice someone unexpectedly. We can acknowledge and welcome their presence or ignore them. There are times when we could have been in a quiet place minding our business or just resting, then suddenly, someone called our name, walked by, startled us, or sat nearby without being noticed. We thought we were alone, but someone else was present. Our emotions were possibly relieved, agitated or exasperated.

INVOCATION

Father God, I come before You in the Powerful name of Jesus the Christ, Your Son and our Savior and Lord. Thank You, Father, for You alone have created all things and have caused these words to be written for such a TIME AS THIS! I come asking You, Father, that You would consecrate the words of this Your servant, Dana R. Johnson, as they are written in this book, which is dedicated to the work You have performed in her life. You, O Lord, are the orchestrator of this life altering account. You, O Lord, are the lifter of her head and the foundation for which these WORDS were penned. Father, I ask that You consecrate this printed work, that it may reach the hearts and souls of those who will read and meditate upon the manifestation of a heart that longs to experience the joy of Your presence. Father, I ask that HE, THE HOLY SPIRIT, WOULD speak to the mind, body, souls, and spirit of all those whose eyes will read and experience the journey of what it means to be Set Apart. In the powerful and matchless Name of Jesus, thank You, Father. Have Your way as these words begin to change lives and restore the hope of all who read "Set-pa-ration." AMEN.

Prepared by Minister Chandra Stevens Atkins

INTRODUCTION

"Keep your thoughts continually fixed on all that is authentic and real, honorable and admirable, beautiful and respectful, pure and holy, merciful and kind. And fasten your thoughts on every glorious work of God, praising him always"
(Philippians 4:8 TPT).

When experiencing a low and imbalanced state of mind, loud thoughts can replay and make one believe they are useless, unloved and friendless. Emotional thoughts that say, "All I want," "I do not have anyone," "No one wants to be around me," "No one cares about me," and "I do not have friends." Those thoughts are negative, toxic, unhealthy, and are not true. Many unwanted emotional circumstances, such as periods of separation, distance or loss of loved ones, trigger damage to the mind and emotions. Negative thoughts and negative emotions are obstacles, which hinder progress and development, resulting in loneliness, reduced effectiveness, sadness, and depression.

Loneliness is a low state of mind that disconnects people from existing in truth and reality—the living world. One is senseless of care and love for others and mindless of the fact that they are not living alone and the loud thoughts are lies. There was a point in my life when I was lonely. Disregarding my feelings and concealing my sorrow and anguish kept me from being content with my life until self-discovery. Self-centered urges impeded my constant faith and trust, and caused me to lose sight of my goals and identity. I wasn't thriving and my spirit withered. My emotional actions prevented me from living a fulfilling and productive life. Being someone who knows the Lord and has been a devoted servant in the church, I was confused about my direction, aspirations and whom to confide in. I needed divine intervention to guide me and enlighten my understanding of my circumstances. I had to examine myself, delve deep and find the strength to push past hurt and pain.

I allowed society to influence my perspective on life instead of adhering to the desire and Will of the Lord. I did not shield my heart from effects that I did not have control over. I frequently prioritized external pressures and expectations over my trust in God's work. The uncontrollable circumstances skewed my sense of time and I succumbed to complacency, remaining unaware. My lack of awareness of how my emotions hindered my motivation led to delay and stagnation. I did not have the strength or mental capacity to push through the pain. During a time meant for growth and prosperity, uncontrollable occurrences led me to feel disappointment, abandonment, unworthiness, and shamefulness. My experience was one of powerlessness, uselessness and shame, which exacerbated emotional pain into my heart and fear in my mind.

Who am I? Where am I? Why do I exist? In my mind, a little girl's dream started "once upon a time" and concluded with a positive outcome. Divine intervention saved me. He pulled me from the bottom of what seemed like an ocean. My soul sank until His hand rescued me.

> *"…You've stayed long enough at this mountain.*
> *On your way now. Get moving…"*
> (Deuteronomy 1:6-7 MSG).

Driven to leave a stagnant and isolated environment, I found the courage to move to a place of acceptance, hope and encouragement. My perspective on life shifted when I grasped what I needed to discover: hope and strength through my belief.

3

Set-pa-ration (Setparation) is my definition for a set time of separation for the Lord. Set-pa-ration is a time, by God's design, that separated me for Him from people and selective choices of the world. It was a period of letting go of my will to remove idols of time and space for pursuance and walking in the true revelation of God. It was a moment of spiritual healing and strengthening to enrich and bless my soul.

Unaware of my identity, unfamiliar with the extent of my capabilities or the power of my beliefs, dreadful and unsettling ideas invaded my mind, diminishing my ability to move and feel optimistic and self-assured. Time passed before I understood the necessity of protecting my emotions. Visualization of dreaded events from reading material and media drama became a place of fear in my heart. Painful and troubling thoughts entered my mind, distorted my vision and stimulated emotional responses. I lived with negative feelings and feared shame. I did not want to accept the events or what was beyond my influence. My selfish desires blinded me—perishing and not prospering—but now understanding dawns. My refusal to accept or approve of what occurred in my life clouded my spirit, overwhelming me with false hope and doubt. I became lost and alienated from reality.

In Isaiah 42:16 (NIV), God said, *"I will lead the blind by ways they have not known, along unfamiliar paths I will guide them; I will turn the darkness into light before them and make the rough places smooth. These are the things I will do; I will not forsake them."* The Lord did what He said He would do.

Throughout the chapters, I share the truth about loneliness, unfolding what I buried and hid within. Ever since the Lord rescued and saved me, I have persistently avoided entanglement in thoughts and emotions and continued to walk in total victory and freedom.

CHAPTER 1

STATE OF LONELINESS

*"The soul that sees beauty may
sometimes walk alone."*
– Johann Wolfgang Von Goethe

A person dealing with loneliness is never alone because a person who is alone is never alone. Loneliness is a feeling when one has not learned to cope with being apart from others. The feeling becomes a challenge for the mind and intellect. It impacts mental well-being and reduces life's meaning, which often results in the absence of a person or people that can lead to depression and heartache. As a short-term emotional response to depression, loneliness impairs daily functioning. A tendency exists to isolate oneself to keep from exposing sadness, guilt, insensibility, insecurity, and loss of interest when loneliness is a factor.

Loneliness exists in a person's mind and soul and trespasses into one's spirit. The longer one considers being apart and remote from someone, the more awful the prospect seems. Loneliness isolates and snares the mind and causes many to forget their value, worth, positive influences, and close connections triggered by disheartening events that stem from emotional upsets. Distance, loss and disconnection from family, friends and society fuel loneliness. Social relationships become disturbing, dreadful and humiliating. The feeling is that quantity or quality does not meet social needs.

If lonely thoughts are not controlled, they can create space in a person's mind that consumes their soul and causes emotional pain in their heart. Once lonely thoughts take hold, the thoughts sap one's energy to live, thrive and pursue life. Anxiety and anger may grip the heart of one saddened by abandonment, and the mind is not at peace due to judgment and fear of others' perspectives. The mind and heart lose their ability to recognize or acknowledge a support network in this lonely state. The suffering is intense, and the heart grows weary, resulting in impaired judgment, poor decision-making and confusion.

Among adults aged 45 and older, 1-in-3 are lonely. In Loneliness and Social Connections: A National Survey of Adults 45 and Older, AARP research stated that 48 percent of adults who are very and somewhat unsatisfied with their partner are lonely compared to 26 percent who are very or somewhat satisfied.[1] One can experience loneliness with companionship and social relationships.

A 2024 nationally representative survey by Pew Research Center found that women are more adept at coping with life changes and are less vulnerable than men in their relationships with others.[2] Loneliness affects all age groups and is particular to adjusting to the challenges of life's transitions and individual social preferences.[3] It affects adolescents transitioning to adulthood, young adults establishing social and interpersonal relationships, and older adults into the elderly and final stage of life. At some point in every experience, there is some form of loneliness.

The Impact

Loneliness taxes the body because of mental stress. The American Heart Association News (2022) reports that social isolation and loneliness harm heart and brain health. Social isolation has a significant impact that contributes to heart failure, poor brain health, dementia, and cognitive impairment. Uncontrolled emotions of loneliness can lead to chronic health conditions and cause premature death. A strong link is evident between heart disease and stroke, and an increase in heart attacks and strokes is due to loneliness, sadness and depression.[4]

Percentage	Complication
29%	Heart attack/heart disease death
32%	Stroke

Loneliness may contribute to other life-threatening disorders and diseases such as anxiety, anger, hypertension, dementia, Type-2 diabetes, and a weak immune system. There is comfort in knowing that no one is alone. Discovering ways to foster positive emotions is crucial for the well-being and prosperity of one's soul and overall health.

Chapter 2

Mindset

"What you focus on expands, so focus on what you want and not what you do not want."
– Esther Jno Charles

Every problem leads to the hidden truth and discovery of who we are, the place [state of] which we live, the evidence of where we are going, and an encounter that transforms us for the next phase of our lives. Look away from the problem and strive to conquer the challenge.

If the focus is on loneliness, then loneliness is in control. Whatever is in control has total influence over God's plans for our life. It influences actions, behavior and decisions. If a woman feels lonely, then her emotions allude to being alone. But if she thinks and believes she is lonely, she identifies herself as lonely. As a woman thinks in her heart, so is she (Proverbs 23:7). Assume she believes that she cannot succeed without assistance. In that case, she cannot because her thoughts govern her, limits her ability to move beyond her thoughts and shrinks her capacity to get more than she does not have. Giving loneliness permission to control the mind drives the heart to an undesirable state. To avoid a life-ruining destiny, combat loneliness.

Too much attention to loneliness creates a struggle that weakens one's perseverance. If so, loneliness has the power and authority to rule their life. The power of loneliness causes them to refuse to go places and stay isolated. It makes people feel detached and alters their brains, hindering their ability to trust and connect to others.[5] Do not give place to loneliness; we must take possession and control of our thoughts as a deterrence towards isolation, bitterness, or depression and secure peace. If the problem is the driver and the problem is loneliness, then loneliness is the driver. We cannot let preconceived thoughts or notions drive us.

> *"Fear not, for I am with you; Be not dismayed, for I am your God. I will strengthen you, Yes, I will help you, I will uphold you with My righteous right hand"* (Isaiah 41:10 NKJV).

I limited my socialization and interactions with others. I kept up my performance in the workplace to avoid judgment and being looked down on. People labeled me as a well-behaved girl who always behaves appropriately. Aside from a few friends and the church community, I did not recognize the advantages of social interaction. What better perception for people to form of me than to always socialize with believers and hide my pain? I considered what others might comment, fearing a negative impact on my persona.

Romans 12:2 (NKJV) says, *"And do not be conformed to this world, but be transformed by the renewing of your mind, that you may prove what is that good and acceptable and perfect will of God."* I studied the first part of that verse but failed to notice the transformation part. I considered the actions, but my mind remained fixed on the image and perception—the prideful things of life that are part of this world. I weighed the appearance of a good person in the sight of man more than to the heart of the Lord. For it is written in 1 Samuel 16:7 (ESV), *"But the Lord said to Samuel, 'Do not look at his appearance or on the height of his stature, because I have rejected him. For the Lord sees not as man sees; man looks on the outward appearance, but the Lord looks on the heart.'"*

My inner life was withering because I failed to reshape my thoughts to reflect on how the Lord always viewed me. Pressures from things I witnessed and experienced in the past shaped into mental images of other people. This included finding fault in my marriage decision, which introduced me to shame. I shifted my thoughts to prevent the adoption of others' perspectives. So apprehensive about someone's opinion of me, I ignored it and didn't contemplate how the Lord viewed me.

> *"For I know the thoughts that I think toward you, says the Lord, thoughts of peace and not of evil, to give you a future and a hope"*
> (Jeremiah 29:11 NKJV).

I was forced to manage low tolerance, anger and resentment. I did not consider its effect on my health. The state of loneliness affects health conditions, behaviors, and self-identification. In a period of spiritual decline, as my life seemed to crumble, I questioned the sufficiency of my resources. A low place facilitated the return of painful, best-forgotten memories.

Spiritual avoidance caused me to walk away or tune out responses I did not want to hear or receive. Comments and gestures that contradict my hopes, beliefs and opinions emotionally grieved my heart and sent nerve triggers causing me to separate myself and walk away in silence. "How dare one make such

13

an exclaim without knowing the truth or thinking it through." It does not mean that I am not guilty, but it is noticeable to self when emotionally destressed.

I avoided all conversations that could potentially touch upon my concealed internal suffering. That caused me to distance myself from family and friends who offered opinions about my life. I disconnected from anyone who often spoke derogatory of my situations or did not provide the words of counsel I wanted to hear or receive. I did not want to expose my vulnerability, only my strength. I concealed my weakness and ignored advice, though my mental state required guidance for life improvements.

Figuratively, parents permitted their teenaged daughter to drive their car to visit a friend, specifying a nine o'clock curfew and a no-other driver rule. The teen and her friend went to a social event without permission and returned home late. Irrespectively, out of exhaustion and curfew, the teen let her friend drive them to get something to eat. The daughter went against her parents' request and the parents questioned the teen about her disobedience and expressed the risk. The insurance covered the teenager, not the friend to whom the keys were given.

In the same manner, God sent Jesus to save us. Jesus did not die on the cross for loneliness. His sacrifice acted like an insurance policy to cover us. We must not allow challenges to drive us nor allow difficulties to trap us in captivity. Jesus did not die on the cross for challenging issues, but for all to be free. He took the problems to the cross so that we do not have to carry them. He wants to take us to unfamiliar destinations, but He cannot take us if our will is of lonely state.

Whatever we choose or allow to drive us will determine our destiny. If we dislike the route we are on, we need to change the route. We can turn around and go back to our previous location before finding the lonely place. We can return to the state before loneliness ever shadows our mind. Moreover, we can renew our mind in the Spirit (Ephesians 4:23) by *"casting down imaginations, and every high thing that is exalted against the knowledge of God, and bringing every thought into captivity to the obedience of Christ;"* (2 Corinthians 10:5 ASV). If we follow God's Word, we will maintain peace of mind and avoid ever sinking or remaining in a lonely place. We have the power and authority to establish limits and regulations that won't hinder a positive outlook and advancement.

"Finally, believers, whatever is true, whatever is honorable and worthy of respect, whatever is right and confirmed by God's word, whatever is pure and wholesome, whatever is lovely and brings peace, whatever is admirable and of good repute; if there is any excellence, if there is anything worthy of praise, think continually on these things [center your mind on them, and implant them in your heart]" (Philippians 4:8 AMP).

CHAPTER 3

HIDDEN DISCOVERY

"Trust in the Lord with all your heart, And lean
not on your own understanding; In all your ways
acknowledge Him, And He shall direct your paths"
(Proverbs 3:5-6 NKJV).

A maze or labyrinth is a puzzle of convoluted paths mapped on paper. A maze garden is a field where one who enters at one location must find the route to reach their goal of exiting at the other point. It's difficult trying to get through a maze without detouring or restarting because of the convoluted paths. As individuals advance through the various stages, discovering the solution becomes more challenging. A maze drawn on a paper course may be easier to navigate because one can gauge the visibility of all turning points. Only the labyrinth's creator can chart the routes and understand which routes are blocked and how to proceed from the entrance to the exits. Navigating a maze without overhead visibility presents significant challenges and fear, particularly when numerous turns are dead ends, complicated direction selection and necessitating careful step-by-step navigation. Those navigating their way through the labyrinth are required to listen to the voice of the one who has oversight and knowledge of where all the paths lead.

Likewise, life is a puzzling maze, a field of many turns and multiple trails that lead to dead ends, with only one way out. To be in a lonely place is a dead end resulting in stagnation and no progress. Instead of remaining in a lonely place, we can choose the correct path. Whenever we do not take the right path, we can retrace our steps from the dead end. After retracting to the last turning point, we can choose another direction.

Life presents challenges at important junctures. At each turning point, obstacles affect one's momentum by triggering emotions and testing their response. Emotions are enjoyment, excitement, gratitude, joy, pleasure, calmness, resentment, grief, shame, guilt, sadness, fear, and anxiety. Obstacles are significant mind triggers causing emotional disturbances that cause and affect one's momentum. If one is weak in emotions, the obstacles may influence the timing of the moment and cause stagnation. While in that stagnant place, they will waste time waiting for others to solve their life challenges.

The mind triggers can stir up emotions, drawing feelings of alienation, being misled by pain, and feeling alone and misunderstood. Some triggers result from a combination of experiences that started in childhood. Mind-triggering obstacles could lead to isolation. The opposing advantage of isolation is the growing emotion of not being loved, growing empty and not fulfilled. One may arrive at a place where being alone and silent is alright. The silent keeper's internal struggles are often a mystery.

I learned to cope and be content with my life and live behind emotional silence. I learned to repress all the emotional pain from feelings and thoughts that no one understood my experiences, causing me to withdraw. I avoided acknowledging my submersion. I realized that even though connected to people and family, one could hide and drown in emotional pain. This impacts how a person masks and carries themselves. This prevents them from being true to themselves and sincere.

Determining the correct routes independently might appear unattainable. However, with the leading of the Holy Spirit, life is less complicated. The decisions and actions of individuals can lead to dead ends. When driven by a personal desire to navigate difficult situations and minimize suffering, they could give the impression of being alone and unsupported.

I doubt anyone should navigate life without companionship. Gauging points exist at every turn and through every circumstance. One should be acquainted with the directional gauges in times of fear, loss, aloneness, and challenges. However, when trying to overcome difficulty, a cry out from the heart with a desire to seek help from the Lord, the One who saves, will be heard and He will lead the way for anyone who seeks Him.

For it is written, *"Where there is no guidance, a people falls, but in an abundance of counselors there is safety"* (Proverbs 11:14 ESV). God is waiting for our call and a time to commune. Listen to and follow the Lord. In His response, He says, *"But the one who always listens to me will live undisturbed in a heavenly peace. Free from fear, confident and courageous, that one will rest unafraid and sheltered from the storms of life"* (Proverbs 1:33 TPT).

Questions: Recall a setback from a significant event that impacted your objective for accomplishing a goal. What emotions did you feel?

_____

_____

_____

When you considered the objective, what outcome were you anticipating?

_____

_____

_____

What constituted that goal and what was the importance?

_____

_____

_____

Does the desire to accomplish the goal still exist?

_____

_____

_____

How does considering the goal make you feel?

_____

_____

_____

Do you trust the Lord to regain proper direction?

_____

_____

_____

*"To You, O LORD, I lift my soul; in You, my God,
I trust. Do not let me be put to shame; do not let
my enemies exult over me. Surely none who wait
for You will be put to shame; but those who are
faithless without cause will be disgraced. Show me
Your ways, O LORD; teach me Your paths. Guide
me in Your truth and teach me, for You are the
God of my salvation; all day long I wait for You.
Remember, O LORD, Your compassion and loving
devotion, for they are from age to age. Remember
not the sins of my youth, nor my rebellious acts;
remember me according to Your loving devotion,
because of Your goodness, O LORD. Good and
upright is the LORD; therefore He shows sinners
the way. He guides the humble in what is right and*

teaches them His way. All the LORD's ways are loving and faithful to those who keep His covenant and His decrees. For the sake of Your name, O LORD, forgive my iniquity, for it is great. Who is the man who fears the LORD? He will instruct him in the path chosen for him. His soul will dwell in prosperity, and his descendants will inherit the land. The LORD confides in those who fear Him, and reveals His covenant to them. My eyes are always on the LORD, for He will free my feet from the mesh. Turn to me and be gracious, for I am lonely and afflicted. The troubles of my heart increase; free me from my distress. Consider my affliction and trouble, and take away all my sins. Consider my enemies, for they are many, and they hate me with vicious hatred. Guard my soul and deliver me; let me not be put to shame, for I take refuge in You. May integrity and uprightness preserve me, because I wait for You. Redeem Israel, O God, from all its distress" (Psalm 25:1-22 BSB).

CHAPTER 4

SHIFTING FOCUS

You are who you believe yourself to be.
You possess what you claim. Declare it.
You get what you meditate and speak on.

Emotional abandonment started in my childhood and progressed into adulthood and marriage. It was a mountain barrier that caused insecurity, provoked disheartening, and made me feel uncared for and unloved. I experienced loneliness whether alone or with others. That's not physical abandonment, but rather a deficiency in emotional awareness.

Emotional abandonment is when a parent or caregiver does not meet a child's emotional needs for support, love or validation. Symptoms of emotional abandonment are deceptive and cause one to believe they are being ignored and overlooked and unmindful of others. People who deal with emotional abandonment unknowingly desert their feelings and emotions and have insecurity concerns.

Instances existed when I embraced loneliness with a negative awareness, letting my feelings dominate and fill my spirit with disappointment, dejection, sadness, shame, and embarrassment. During such times, I lacked the desire to confide in anyone except my spouse. I only trusted a few and limited what I shared with others. I subtly addressed it depending on his availability and openness to my concerns.

My ex-husband always proved the best choice to listen to and answer anything I faced mentally, emotionally, socially, and physically. I expected him to resolve whatever I needed and put all my concerns at ease, but when he did not, I felt he did not care. I wanted him there when I needed him, even in difficult times. I learned that expecting him to balance my life mentally, emotionally, socially, and physically was very selfish.

I expected the same attentiveness from my parents. I recall crying whenever I did not get the attention I wanted. I would go into hiding or pretend to have run away or attempt suicide. I expected more from my parents than they could afford and didn't notice their stress. I perceived life from what I required, not from the world's evolution around me.

It was extremely difficult to overcome emotional abandonment and dissolve self-limitations. I knew my actions did not please God when I sought gratification and glory for myself. However, one day, I began to perceive my behavior through others. I understood its nature and disliked the sight. I believed in Christ while seeking empathy and having self-pity to gain attention and support from others.

I experienced mental burnout and stress trying to fix the imperfections in things to appear correct for a perfected outlook. Recognizing the time passage and my own lack of progress, I changed my concentration. I needed to turn away and humble myself. I was concerned with others' opinions and rarely attended social events that influenced competence, confidence and performance. The effect on me was both beneficial and detrimental. I needed to internally battle and subdue every arrogant thought exceeding God's knowledge and wisdom, forcing all thinking to follow Christ (2 Corinthians 10:5). It was necessary for me to decide on the courses in my life to shift my focus from a lonely, oppressive state to an expansive and lively state. I realized that I did not need the constant approval of a man or woman.

I sacrificed so much battling life's repetitions that I refused to endure it further. The space I gave to loneliness, shame, rejection, doubt, fear, and rejection needed addressing.

"For assuredly, I say to you, whoever says to this mountain, 'Be removed and be cast into the sea,' and does not doubt in his heart, but believes that those things he says will be done, he will have whatever he says. Therefore I say to you, whatever things you ask when you pray, believe that you will receive them, and you will have them"
(Mark 11:23-24 NKJV).

Fear of Being Alone

Spiritual realization is knowing and understanding that humans are body, mind, soul, and spirit, and believing that the Spirit of the Lord and His presence is with them. All who have faith in the Lord must accept the Lord's presence. He declared, "I'll always be with you and support you." The Lord does not abandon but rescues. Jesus did everything He said He would do when He walked the earth before His crucifixion. His Words exclude nothing and He disrespects no one. Believe in Him and use His Word to adopt an unfamiliar perspective. Meditate on God's Word, both day and night, to discipline the mind by renewing it. Start with praying this prayer, which includes 2 Kings 6:17, Psalm 119:18 and Psalm 91:15:

Lord, please open my spiritual eyes so that I may see and notice that there are more hosts with me than obstacles and challenges against me. Father, open my eyes that I may behold wondrous things out of Your law. Lord, I know that when I call on You, You will answer. Please help me to overcome my fear of moments of being alone. I know You will be with me in trouble and deliver me in Jesus' Name, Amen.

Some expectations can be burdensome to others, and expecting someone to carry and discard another's weight when the burden is not theirs is selfish. We may encounter helpful people, but no one is obligated to alleviate our burden. After praying for God to open our spiritual eyes, we must relinquish our burdens to Jesus. Put it all in His hand. The load is an internal, spiritual battle we do not have to carry. Thus, we should not retrieve the matter once we have relinquished it to Jesus. Although this is easier said than done, it is a self-regulating procedure. Jesus said, "Pick up your cross and follow me" (Matthew 16:24). All we must do is obey His command.

What may appear harmful or threatening to life is only fear. The fear creates thoughts and an emotional apprehensiveness of being alone. The fear of letting go; the fear of not knowing how to survive; the fear of having to live without a spouse, dear loved one, or close relative; the fear of being alone in a place where we once had a friend or a companion; the fear of traveling to or dwelling in a new place alone.

Fear arises from a lack of confidence in one's capacity for success and well-being in solitude. Autophobia is a specific phobia or morbid fear of being alone, isolated, abandoned, and ignored. This type of fear limits one's ability to pursue goals and aspirations without the help of someone else. We must let go of our dependency on man and grow in faith, relying on God. Faith is the instrument of our feet, the rhythm in our steps, orchestrated by our heart. Faith is an act of movement that overrides fear. Fear occurs when our eyes are not on God and not focused on the promise. Without faith, we cannot please God.

> *"fear not, for I am with you; be not dismayed, for I am your God; I will strengthen you, I will help you, I will uphold you with my righteous right hand"* (Isaiah 41:10 ESV).

Questions:

What role does fear play in your life when it comes to being alone?

_____

_____

_____

To what extent are you willing to give space to fear of being alone?

_____

_____

_____

Do you remember when you first felt alone and how that affected you?

_____

_____

_____

What was the outcome of that feeling and do you remember conquering it? Did a similar experience ever happen again?

_____

_____

_____

Did you grow up in a family structure home where your initial departure stemmed from college or the military?

_____

_____

_____

Was the emotion present linked to any other sense of detachment, loss or emptiness?

_____

_____

_____

Do you ever recall being in a place where your parents/guardian left you in the care of someone else and you did not want to stay? If so, did you sense desertion or did you feel reassured that they would return soon?

_____

_____

_____

_____

_____

Was it easy for you to regroup and interact with the person your parents entrusted your care, or did you wander off to be alone?

_____

_____

_____

_____

If you are/were married, did you leave home and go straight into marriage or did you pursue a career away from home before marriage?

_____

_____

_____

_____

Were any of your childhood experiences and emotions like your adulthood experience and emotion?

_____

_____

_____

_____

If so, as an adult, how would you respond to the emotions your childhood-self experienced and felt?

_____

_____

_____

_____

"Arise, for this matter is your responsibility. We also are with you. Be of good courage, and do it"
(Ezra 10:4 NKJV).

CHAPTER 5

RENEWED MIND

"Do not conform to the patterns of this world, but be transformed by the renewing of your mind. Then you will be able to test and approve what God's will is—his good, pleasing and perfect will"
(Romans 12:2 NIV).

Spiritual bondage is a spiritual imprisonment of the mind that separates one from life and reality. Loneliness can distort one's reality, giving the impression that they are lost in a nonexistent world. Emotions and feelings create blocks for the mind's thoughts. Spiritual blocks in the mind keep one from knowing the truth, using faith tools, and accessing keys to their victory. A negative mindset considers the old while hoping and expecting something new or better blocks the new and better from manifesting. Negative patterns are a debt of learned habits that restrict progress toward change.

*"Those who are motivated by the flesh only pursue
what benefits themselves. But those who live by the
impulses of the Holy Spirit are motivated to pursue
spiritual realities. For the sense and reason of the
flesh is death, but the mind-set controlled by the
Spirit finds life and peace. In fact, the mind-set
focused on the flesh fights God's plans and refuses
to submit to his direction, because it cannot!"*
(Romans 8:5-7 TPT).

Most tend to focus their attention on what is observable. Instead, we must focus on what is desired. Mark 11:24 (NET) says, *"For this reason I tell you, whatever you pray and ask for, believe that you have received it, and it will be yours."* Allowing the past and present trauma to consume our mind will restrict us from creating space for the future. Permitting emotions concerning the intangible or absent from social interaction to dominate our mind and thoughts eliminates future hope. The future is not in past trauma, hurt or pain, but trauma, hurt and pain in the past requires healing to receive the promised future. Outside of negative mentalities and emotional wounds, the future is beyond images of hurt and insufficiency.

The physical body has multiple senses. Romans 8:5 says, "Those who are motivated by the flesh only pursue what benefits themselves." The reason behind loneliness is that someone or others are wanted and are motivated by the flesh. We can stand and live beyond the arms of a loved one. Those who are perusing this book can overcome any obstacle by changing their thoughts and perspective on a significant emotional experience.

Confining sensory experience to touch undermines the brain and encourages responses from other physical senses. Anyone who focuses on who and what is not available for their desire misses the opportunity to seep into spaces and events for growth and expansion.

In the Kingdom of God, there are seasons where God will take us through growth and expansion. Growth comes with multiplication; before we can expand, we must go through a growth process. God builds us up before He stretches us. Growth is going and springing in an upward movement, a reach in our developing process. Growth is a building process and expansion is adding to what is available. We grow in knowledge, understanding, wisdom, and strength, but He stretches us within our faith.

We can want more, but God must develop us first. What God develops will make room for what is necessary to expand. God wants us to be able to uphold what He springs through us. Once He develops and establishes us in an area (position, stage or location), He starts to stretch us, and then there is a pruning process for more growth and expansion. He deals with our weaknesses, failures and bad habits.

As an illustration, when tomato seeds are planted in soil, there is a growth process. First, a stem starts to sprout from a seed. Once the stem reaches a particular height and tomatoes grow from the blooms, the gardener lays the vine downward underneath the soil. The vine is stretched outward and buried underneath the soil for expansion. From the stretched vine, more vines sprout, creating a wider spread. If the gardener did not lay the first growth in the soil, the vine would continue to reach upward but never create any room to expand, and the weight of tomatoes growing on the vine would be overbearing. Stretching the vine promotes the capacity necessary for multiplication to produce. It would not have the capacity to hold and produce at its fullest without the gardener laying down the stem.

Renewing the mind is a step in the unknown, inexperienced, spiritual and natural relational concepts. It benefits the soul by bringing new order to mind senses and shifts the focus. What is not correct, irrelevant or limiting is cached out for the download of new knowledge, which will cause an expansion in conscious thinking and fill it with the truth. It is surrendering one's thoughts and opening one's mind for the Lord to reveal and reposition one's thinking. The human mind and reality begin to reshape and reform through confession, forgiveness, repentance, and faith. One's perspective about what they thought that they did not have changes and their spirit is edified and comforted with peacefulness, confidence, reassurance, and elevation. I once was lost, but now I am found because Christ saved me.

The first step of having a renewed mind is believe that God loves us so much that He sent His only Son so that everyone who believes in Him will not perish but have eternal life (John 3:16). And His only Son died on the cross to atone for all sins and rose from the grave in three days. One's mind is the eyes of their reality.

It is easy to be comforted by the company of others, but it is best to be consoled with peace, knowing that God is forever present. There are many traps and challenging places in life, but He hears and saves when we call on Jesus. The Lord saves us from the snares of negative thoughts, fear, pain, trauma, rape, molestation, abuse, the wrath of the wicked, ill-spoken words, traps of the enemy, and loneliness. Through faith and my words of confessing, He restored me.

<u>Confession Prayer</u>:

I believe Jesus is Lord and believe in my heart that God raised Him from the dead in three days. Thank You for sending Your Son, Jesus Christ, to die for my sins. Forgive me for my sins. I invite You into my heart to save me. In Jesus' Name, Amen.

CHAPTER 6

SET APART

"For if you keep silent at this time, relief and deliverance will arise for the Jews from another place, but you and your father's house will perish. And who knows whether you have not come to the kingdom for such a time as this?"
(Esther 4:14 ESV).

The journey of being set apart deepened my desire for fulfillment, companionship, partnership, and love. My military career assignments frequently separated me from my family for short and long periods, causing emotional hardship. The desire for connection and touch was limited and, in my heart, I felt empty. When I was pregnant with my first daughter, I thought having a baby would change my life and fill my heart. After giving birth, my life changed, but she did not fulfill what was missing, nor did the subsequent pregnancy and delivery. I received promotions and awards and did everything right, living a good yet unfulfilled life.

I had an incredible support system from neighbors, family and childcare. I always had everything I needed around me and from afar. I was thankful and genuinely grateful for my circle of love. Frankly, from the physical eye, I lacked nothing besides my years apart from my husband while I was married. Even in those times, I gained wisdom, knowledge, friendship, skills, and understanding. Like Jesus told the disciples in John 13:7 (NIV), *"You do not realize now what I am doing, but later you will understand."* I could not understand until I started having intimate time with the Father in Heaven. Life's puzzle has many pieces, but we will see the design when every intended part and turning in our lives is in place.

My mind had me trapped, feeling alone. When and if I opened my heart to share my feelings, family and friends looked at me as if I were out of my right mind. There was no apprehension of the truth to what I was living with. The outside view of my life conflicted with what I was processing in my mind.

I did not know or recognize who I was, feeling emotionally abandoned and lost in a world unrecognizable to the people who surrounded me. I was numb to the effects of socialism and celebrating life. I was taking up space on Earth by existing but not

41

living. I did not have a sense of fulfillment, although I was actively involved in my church community, had my family and friends, and loved the fellowship of the Lord. I suppressed my emotions, only existing and not living. I had not recovered from the mountainous barriers of past hurt and pain, rejection, abandonment, and loneliness, which are attached to depression and oppression. I had to wake up.

> *"Wake up! Strengthen what remains and is about to die, for I have found your deeds unfinished in the sight of my God. Remember, therefore, what you have received and heard; hold it fast, and repent. But if you do not wake up, I will come like a thief, and you will not know at what time I will come to you"* (Revelation 3:2-3 NIV).

The Rising

I recall going to a women's retreat and writing everything I desired the Lord to free me from on paper. As the women prayed and worshiped, we nailed to a cross all the words, requests and pain by canceling the record of debt that stood against us with its legal demands. Then, the minister carried the cross to a fire pit, a sign to be destroyed forever in faith.

"And you, who were dead in your trespasses and the uncircumcision of your flesh, God made alive together with him, having forgiven us all our trespasses, by canceling the record of debt that stood against us with its legal demands. This he set aside, nailing it to the cross. He disarmed the rulers and authorities and put them to open shame, by triumphing over them in him"
(Colossians 2:13-15 ESV).

There was a spiritual release in the atmosphere. Everything we were holding on to had to disarm its hold on our lives. Without faith to believe, what took place in nature was an outward expression of what we needed to release in our hearts. If not, captivity would remain Resurrection and liberation only happened once I desired and believed. There was forgiving, healing, delivering, resurrecting, and liberation to the level of thinking in the power of faith.

"that if you confess with your mouth the Lord Jesus and believe in your heart that God has raised Him from the dead, you will be saved. For with the heart one believes unto righteousness, and with the mouth confession is made unto salvation"
(Romans 10:9-10 NKJV).

This is the promise of salvation that brings hope. The confession to receive the gift of salvation is a step in the doorway of Heaven through Christ Jesus. For it is written, *"Jesus saith unto him, I am the way, the truth, and the life: no man cometh unto the Father, but by me"* (John 14:6). Acknowledging that Jesus Christ died on the cross and rose in three days was a statement of confession from my heart. I believe in Him, and because I believe, I gained total access to the Father in Heaven. The resurrected power that is Christ Jesus awakened in my heart.

> *"Since you have been raised to new life with Christ, set your sights on the realities of heaven, where Christ sits in the place of honor at God's right hand. Think about the things of heaven, not the things of earth. For you died to this life, and your real life is hidden with Christ in God. And when Christ, who is your life, is revealed to the whole world, you will share in all his glory"*
> (Colossians 3:1-4 NLT).

Christ's resurrection is our resurrection too. The life we live with Christ is now. The Bible says, *"The Spirit of God, who raised Jesus from the dead, lives in you. And just as God raised Christ Jesus from the dead, he will give life to your mortal bodies by this same Spirit living within you"* (Romans 8:11 NLT). The power to save and resurrect became alive in me, but I still had sinful things in my life that required deliverance. The gift of salvation continually requires faith. The grace to save and deliver was upon me, but I had to learn how to walk it out.

Understanding His Grace

Although the grace of salvation was upon me, and Jesus' sacrifice opened the door to spiritual freedom, I was not free. I was still dealing with bondage and spiritual blocks. Water baptism and the gift of the Holy Spirit did not bring complete fulfillment. There were things in me, which remained in my heart, that God had to reveal for healing and deliverance. I learned that confessing salvation is not a one-time confession.

Realizing there was more to life and spirituality than what I understood, I repeated the prayer of salvation whenever I was in church and heard the call. As I channeled my thoughts to the cross and engaged my heart while reciting the prayer, God drew me closer and I saw the release of sin fall off me in the Spirit. The more I engaged in the prayer of salvation for sanctification, the more God revealed the unfolding of salvation in my life: sanctification and purification. He washed and cleansed me and stripped the pain and weight off my back.

"God has united you with Christ Jesus. For our benefit God made him to be wisdom itself. Christ made us right with God; he made us pure and holy, and he freed us from sin"
(1 Corinthians 1:30 NLT).

Prayer of Faith:

Lord, thank You for the power You have given me to control my thoughts, bind sad and lonely thoughts, and release every negative and drowning mood. With mustard seed faith, I can move mountains that are blocking me from evolving. With You, Lord, I can do all things. I am no longer intimidated and paranoid about the thoughts I think people have of me. The Holy Spirit, not emotional triggers, leads my renewed mind. I cast down every imagination that says I am lonely. I am not alone, for I know You, Lord, are with me everywhere I go. My mind remains at peace, for the Holy Spirit guides me. I am set apart. In the night's stillness, Father, speak to my heart, fill me with Your love, and remind me of Your goodness and the plans You have for me. In Jesus' Name, Amen.

Meditate and consider this: I was born for such a time; set apart to discover my internal self, gain knowledge, wisdom and understanding, and activate the Lord's Will and His purpose for my life.

CHAPTER 7

DISCOVERED IDENTITY

*"People perish from a lack of knowledge and
ignorance of faith, self and society."*

There may be times when we ask ourselves, "Who I am?" or "What am I to God?" The desire to know the answer may persuade some to research their family history and genetic makeup to perform a DNA trace of their bloodline to discover their origin. For those who are seeking the answers, set-pa-ration is a beautiful time to start.

Set-pa-ration is a time by God's design to separate one for God from people and choices of the world. It's the moment to remove idols of time and pursuance and walk in the true revelation of God. It is a juncture for the Lord to pull one away to learn of Him and build a relationship, confidence and trust in Him. It is a time of serenity and rests in Him—to dwell in the presence of the Lord and beneath His wings. Set-pa-ration to get in His face, grow in the Spirit, and learn of ourselves and who we are in Him. It is a time of strengthening, healing, deliverance, and prayer with the Lord. A consecration period for the Lord to fill our heart and discover our true, profound love. Set-pa-ration is set apart with space and God from others to prepare the heart, mind, body, and spirit for a time such as this and this very purpose. Set-pa-ration is a set time of separation for the Lord.

A person with a deceived mind underestimates their value and self-worth when measuring themselves by their company and appearance compared to others. Our true value and self-worth are identified through God and His Word. The Bible tells us, *"We do not dare to classify or compare ourselves with some who commend themselves. When they measure themselves by themselves and compare themselves with themselves, they are not wise"* (2 Corinthians 10:12 NIV).

Antonella Trotta, a clinical psychologist and psychoanalyst, shared that paranoia is fear that threatens one's identity or sense of reason and thoughts. [6] It can manifest fear of being watched critically and judged, thinking people are talking about one behind their back.

"In the multitude of my [anxious] thoughts within me, Your comforts cheer and delight my soul!"
(Psalm 94:19 AMPC).

Apart from Christ, not knowing who I am spiritually made it much easier to get trapped in a mind living in fear, shame and abandonment. *"For God will never give you the spirit of fear, but the Holy Spirit who gives you mighty power, love, and self-control"* (2 Timothy 1:7 TPT). I was trapped in loneliness until I learned who I truly am. But with the help of the Lord, I can do all things. I was like the blind man Jesus had taken out of town, away from his friends, and used spittle to heal his sight in Mark 8:22-26 (NASB), which says:

> *"And they came to Bethsaida. And some people brought a man who was blind to Jesus and begged Him to touch him. Taking the man who was blind by the hand, He brought him out of the village; and after spitting in his eyes and laying His hands on him, He asked him, 'Do you see anything?' And he looked up and said, 'I see people, for I see them like trees, walking around.' Then again He laid His hands on his eyes; and he looked intently and was restored, and began to see everything clearly. And He sent him to his home, saying, 'Do not even enter the village.'"*

The righteous beings are compared to a tree in Psalm 1:3 (ESV), *"He is like a tree planted by streams of water that yields its fruit in its season, and its leaf does not wither. In all that he does, he prospers."* I did not grasp the spiritual connection to my physical life. When depressed, I realized I was missing spiritual fulfillment and was not growing. The truth is, I am one with Christ.

Imagine a tree, which the gardener buries in the soil next to a river. The tree is full of beautiful branches and leaves. A branch cut from a tree withers and gathers to burn away. The tree is Christ, the gardener is the Father and the branches are the believers. He is the vine and I am a branch. Christ laid down His life that I may be born in Him. I am rooted in Him; His roots run through me and are the extension of my lifeline. Detached from Him, I have no life, but I am living, breathing and growing through Him. I am like a tree planted by the water whose leaves do not wither. Attached to Him, I am an extension of everything in Christ. What He bears, I bear. I am He and He is me. (See John 15:1-6.)

I was living to exist on the outside but dying on the inside, a dead woman walking before Christ revealed my hidden self-discovery beyond the knowledge of human comprehension. Until then, I was perishing for lack of spiritual wisdom and divine truth about my internal identity. Subsequently, I stopped looking at myself and others as human beings and started seeing people as spiritual beings serving a spiritual purpose.

The Book of Romans in the Holy Bible was one of my favorites and was my go-to book when stationed overseas in the military. It brought so much insight into how humans are in spirit vs. the flesh. It changed my entire perspective of how I saw life, governing people, and the response to life. I was praying and asking God to help change my situation because the life I had was not my desire. Truthfully, my desires and wants had nothing to do with my flesh but my spirit.

Imagine our internal spirit as an invisible body. In saying so, my spirit man rubbed on my belly for attention and longing to fellowship with me. I was reacting out of my spirit but trying to combat it physically. I was trying to satisfy my spirit out of the flesh.

The sustainment and fulfillment I needed had nothing to do with physical impact but what is internal. Whenever I ask God for something, I ask Him to meet my needs in the Spirit in hopes of a physical manifestation. For it is written, *"Those who live according to the flesh have their minds set on what the flesh desires; but those who live in accordance with the*

Spirit have their minds set on what the Spirit desires" (Romans 8:5 NIV).

Through the years, God unveiled the truths about my identity in those moments of revelation. He showed me the unique person I am, profoundly shaping my personal spiritual journey. I realized I was unaware of my identity in Him; I did not see who I was or my reason for existence. I only knew myself, my purpose and my assignment once I grew and matured in His Word.

I searched within and asked the Holy Spirit to guide, lead and help unfold the layers of my conscious mind. I desired to know who I am and why He sent me. I had to overcome traumatic memories with grace and forgiveness, get beyond others' impressions and perceptions of me, and abolish personal insecurities, fear and jealousy. I had to forget the untruths of others to discover the truth about myself. Spiritual blocks were hindering my progression toward the fullness of abundant living forever.

In the wonders of one night, while sleeping, God gave me visions of my life in the Spirit. There were many things I did not understand, and I am still discovering more about myself. But I know this is how I lived, separate from who I am. My life in the physical only reveals me to the world. In partiality, to some, I am unrecognizable because He discloses and shields me from what is comprehendible to others.

Like our Abba, Father in Heaven, Jesus the Holy Spirit, we are hosts of spiritual beings. For it is written, *"Then God said, 'Let Us make man in Our image, according to Our likeness…So God created man in His own image; in the image of God, He created him; male and female He created them. Then God blessed them…"* (Genesis 1:27-28 NKJV).

The genuine reflection of who we are is underneath the garments of the pain, trauma, molestation, rape, abuse, grief, and obstacles we went through. The truth of our identity is behind the veil, the covering of shame, abuse, abandonment, rejection, and loneliness. Let us remove the veil and worldly coverings that hide the shame, exposing our spiritual nakedness.

The element of a woman is not in her outer apparel, makeup, jewelry, money, position, or title. It is her spiritual [internal] makeup and garments. It is how she wears the Word of God around her neck. It is the clothing of righteousness. It is the shoeing of the gospel upon her feet. It is her helmet of salvation and shield of faith to display His splendor.

"And that the women would also pray with clean hearts, dressed appropriately and adorned modestly and sensibly, not flaunting their wealth. But they should be recognized instead by their beautiful deeds of kindness, suitable as one who worships God" (1 Timothy 2:9-10 TPT).

"…Do not look on his appearance or on the height of his stature, because I have rejected him. For the Lord sees not as man sees: man looks on the outward appearance, but the Lord looks on the heart" (1 Samuel 16:7 ESV).

"Stand therefore, having fastened on the belt of truth, and having put on the breastplate of righteousness, and, as shoes for your feet, having put on the readiness given by the gospel of peace. In all circumstances take up the shield of faith…and take the helmet of salvation, and the sword of the Spirit, which is the word of God,"
(Ephesians 6:14-17 ESV).

Self-Discovery

To get to the place of self-discovery and better understand who we are in Christ as a spiritual being, we must do a self-examination and self-assessment of ourselves and our character. Then, we can pursue the following steps:

1. Remove the articles that cause us to compare ourselves to another person.

We are fearfully and wonderfully made (Psalm 139). We may have similar characteristics to others, but each one of us is unique in design, like snowflakes. Though there are many snowflakes, the design of each one is different from the other. God sends every flake to show His splendor in snow, His beauty in the blizzard. God has assigned us to know a life-giving purpose for God-centered praise (Isaiah 55:10). To know and understand who we are, we must seek our salvation with fear and trembling and find our identity in Christ.

2. Remove the articles that hide and destroy us.

Forgive anyone who hurt, took advantage, and discredited our value. As we walk through removing spiritual destruction, do not keep it private but find someone whom we can trust and who will pray with us unto confession unto them. Look inside to see what God sees when He looks at our heart.

3. Remove character traits and bad habits picked up from someone else and out of rebellion.

What does it mean to be authentic to oneself? If we adapt to the ways of someone admiral, they have become an idol. It is contrary to the way and Will of God to emulate an idol in words and actions that do not represent nor reflect the Kingdom of God and His character, therefore turning away. God predestined us to be conformed to the image of His Son, that He might be the firstborn among many brothers and sisters (Romans 8:28).

4. Remove hatred, anger, bitterness, jealousy, and hate toward others.

Let our conduct be without covetousness; be content with the things we have (Hebrews 14:5). Get rid of all moral filth and evil that is so prevalent, and humbly accept the Word planted in us, which can save us (James 1:21). The wisdom that comes from Heaven is first pure; then peace-loving, considerate, submissive, full of mercy and good fruit, impartial and sincere (James 3:17). With all humility and gentleness, with patience, we must bear one another in love, eager to maintain the unity of the Spirit in the bond of peace (Ephesians 4:2-3).

5. Stop looking at self negatively.

Do not be ashamed of who you are. If we confess Christ as Lord and Savior, we are adopted into the Kingdom of God as an heir. There is no greater love than the love of God. *"Who shall separate us from the love of Christ? Shall tribulation, or distress, or persecution, or famine, or nakedness, or danger, or sword?"* (Romans 8:35 ESV).

6. Give an account of self, unhealthy habits and weaknesses.

Undisciplined and uncontrollable actions are offensive to the representation of God. Doing things to get attention is vain and discredits character. There are times and seasons for everything under the sun. Learn when to respond and when to keep quiet. Everyone should be quick to listen, slow to speak and slow to become angry because human anger does not produce the righteousness that God desires (James 1:19-20). God is always speaking but being action-takers and attention-seekers interfere with hearing God's still voice. It can cause one to miss what the Spirit is—the direction and instruction of the Lord. The Spirit helps us in our weakness while waiting for Him to redeem us. Remain humble, exercise patience and self-control, and allow the Holy Spirit to build our character.

7. Repent for steps one through six and any action of unawareness of self-identity.

True repentance and forgiveness are the first steps in discovering our identity and having a Christlike character. With repentance, one turns away from the old way of thinking. Our acceptance is a declaration to develop a holy and righteous character that pleases God and transforms us into Christ. As we allow our mind to be governed by the Spirit to understand the things of Christ and the Kingdom of God, the Holy Spirit can lead us into all truths. These truths are life and peace (Romans 8:8). When we habitually do the things that please God and our mind is set on what honors God, we are walking and living out in our Christlike character.

Ephesians 4:22-24 (TPT) states, *"And he has taught you to let go of the lifestyle of the ancient man, the old self-life, which was corrupted by sinful and deceitful desires that spring from delusions. Now it's time to be made new by every revelation that's been given to you. And to be transformed as you embrace the glorious Christ-within as your new life and live in union with him!..."* When we no longer identify ourselves by actions of the worldly character, operate in humility, and are obedient to the ways and instructions of God, we are taking on the identity as a child of God and a sibling of Christ Jesus. For those whom the Spirit of God leads are the children of God (Romans 8:14). As a woman thinks in her heart, so is she (Proverbs 23:7).

Affirmations

The words spoken are gamechangers. Speak the following words out loud, believe it and receive it:

- ❖ I am an heir to God's heavenly throne; I dress in rich glorious garments of righteousness.
- ❖ Every detail of me shines and reflects God's image and deflects darkness.
- ❖ I am a seed of God's love, reproduced through Christ Jesus. Christ is within me and I am within Him. We are interconnected.

CHAPTER 8

SURRENDERED

*"So then, surrender to God. Stand up to the devil
and resist him and he will flee in agony"*
(James 4:7 TPT).

It is time to come out of the state of loneliness and release shame, sadness, depression, and abandonment. *"For I consider [from the standpoint of faith] that the sufferings of the present life are not worthy to be compared with the glory that is about to be revealed to us and in us!"* (Romans 8:18 AMP). The revealing of God's glory shall come with a heart surrendered to forgiveness, giving grace and openness to receive and hear what God desires.

Surrendering is letting go of appeasing one's flesh, ceasing to impress upon others, and resisting the gratification of lustful desires. It spiritually releases thoughts, erases imaginations and controls things resistant to God's Will. Surrendering to God's control allows Him to move within us for holy positioning and alignment.

I learned to overcome shame and not compare myself to others. It took some time, but after hearing testimonies and others sharing their story of hurt, my confidence increased. I frequently share my story, especially after encountering others with similar problems and experiences. My story is about the desire to be free and have a pure heart.

The world strongly influences lifestyles of trending, lustful and prideful desires. Trying to keep up with the world can be burdensome, but when set apart, as is consecration unto God, things begin to maneuver and shift in the Spirit because growth and development are taking place. Instead of soaking in loneliness, set aside time for a season to set goals, visions and plans. My time for being set apart was governed by time or seasons to grow in wisdom and stature and favor with God and man (Luke 2:52). It was a time of personal and spiritual development that I may receive greater revelation in His knowledge.

God knows His plans for me (Jeremiah 29:11). If I were not preparing and communing to receive from God, I would not be progressing or operating in the positions He planned and set up for my future. The Bible says, *"But know that the LORD has set apart for Himself [and dealt wonderfully with] the godly man [the one of honorable character and moral courage—the one who does right]. The* LORD *hears and responds when I call to Him"* (Psalm 4:3 AMP).

I have peace knowing that my alone time is time set apart for consecration, self-evaluation, self-reflection, and self-development with healing and deliverance. As stated in Romans 5:1-5 (NKJV), *"Therefore, having been justified by faith, we have peace with God through our Lord Jesus Christ, through whom also we have access by faith into this grace in which we stand, and rejoice in hope of the glory of God. And not only that, but we also glory in tribulations, knowing that tribulation produces perseverance; and perseverance, character; and character, hope. Now hope does not disappoint, because the love of God has been poured out in our hearts by the Holy Spirit who was given to us."*

Standing on God's Word has been the strength rooted in my feet. It propels me to run and not grow weary, walk and not faint (Isaiah 40:31). I stand having my waist girded with truth, my heart covered with the breast of righteousness, and my feet shod with preparing the gospel of peace. I do it all in faith, knowing and believing that I can and will continue to quench all the fiery darts of the wicked one (Ephesians 6:14-16). The Word gives me everything I need. It is the source of my liberation victory. I am content knowing that God is faithful, shows His love to me, and sends His Word to renew, keep and strengthen me (Deuteronomy 7:9).

By faith, I echoed God's Word and He performed. He did what He said He would do, so I learned to speak what I desired to see and send the Word wherever needed (Isaiah 55:11). Whenever I needed help, Christ Jesus helped; whenever I needed healing, the Lord healed; whenever I needed relief, I was relieved; whenever I needed deliverance, there was deliverance; when I needed restoration, He restored. And He is still working.

The Word and Spirit of God is power. It is sharper than any two-edged sword. A word received from God pierces deep between the soul and spirit, between joint and marrow. It knows and exposes our innermost thoughts and intents of the heart (Hebrews 4:12).

I know God is faithful to His Word and His Word and does everything that it says (Isaiah 55:11). The Word lives in power (Hebrews 1:3; 4:12). Since the Spirit is of God, I need to receive and allow the Word of God to work in my spirit. I had to hear, read and process the Word until I could see and receive it in my spirit. Joshua 1:8 (NKJV) says, *"This Book of the Law shall not depart from your mouth, but you shall meditate in it day and night, that you may observe to do according to all that is written in it. For then you will make your way prosperous, and then you will have good success."*

Reading the Word of God is a point of recognition. Hearing the Word of God is a point of identification. Receiving the Word of God is a point of transformation. Speaking the Word of God from the heart is activation.

I surrendered time and attention to God for growth and transformation. By hearing the Word through prayer and fasting, my faith and confidence in the Lord increase (Hebrew 11:1). When my thoughts are fixed on the Word and are pleasing, I do what is good, righteous and holy, and it is acceptable to Him (Romans 12:1).

I surrendered to the old ways of thinking; I stand on 2 Corinthians 5:17; I am a new creation through Christ Jesus. My mind is renewed daily and is transforming like the mind of Christ of knowledge, wisdom, power, kindness, and gentleness, and the mind of joy, peace and everlasting love (Galatians 5:22). The Word of God says, *"Behold, I will do a new thing…"* (Isaiah 43:19 NKJV).

Surrendering is not a burden but a liberating act of laying down oneself for God. It is moving aside everything that is right and best for God's glory. It is saying, "Not my will, but Your Will, God" (Luke

22:42). In this act of surrender, we find relief and freedom, knowing that we are in God's hands. The Bible teaches us, *"Laying your life down in tender surrender before the Lord will bring life, prosperity, and honor as your reward"* (Proverbs 22:4 TPT). I surrendered past losses and stand on Joel 2:25-26 (NKJV), *"So I will restore to you the years that the swarming locust has eaten, The crawling locust, The consuming locust, And the chewing locust, My great army which I sent among you."*

Surrendering is laying it down: pain, hurt, wounds, care, justice, sacrifices, and self to God. Surrendering denounces loneliness, shame, rejection, and abandonment (1 Peter 5:7). Surrendering says, "Lord, I give You my heart and every wound and scar for Your love. Lord, I give You my ways, wants, insecurities, and tears—make me new again."

I surrendered to the wounds of the lies and those naysayers and stand on Job 13:15 (NKJV), *"Though He slay me, yet will I trust Him…"* I surrendered my hurt and stood in forgiveness (Matthew 6:12). I stand on Romans 13:8: I owe no man nothing but love. I stand on Ephesians 4:32 to be kind to one another, tenderhearted, forgiving one another, as God in Christ forgave me. I stand on Psalm 55:22 and cast my burden on the Lord, and He will sustain me; He will never permit the righteous to be moved.

I surrendered my failure and areas of defeat to stand on the Word that tells me I am more than a conqueror; vengeance is the Lord, and He will fight the battle (Genesis 4:15; Romans 12:19). I put on the whole armor of God (Ephesians 6:13).

I surrendered loneliness and stood on Hebrews 13:5, which says God will not leave nor forsake me. The Lord's Words fill empty places in my heart (Psalm 63:1). I shall send His Word to every dry place and command it to live (Ezekiel 37:4-5).

God works through our humility, prayer, steadfastness, and faith. I stand on Matthew 5:5 (NKJV), which says, *"Blessed are the meek, For they shall inherit the earth."* I surrender weakness and stand on 2 Corinthians 12:10 (NKJV), which says, *"…For when I am weak, then I am strong."*

When the heart is not right, God can fix it (Psalm 34:18). With heartbreaks, God can heal it (Psalm 147:3). We cannot see beyond the unknown so we must trust Him because Jesus already went before us. His thoughts are of peace and hope; to prosper for us in all things and be in good health, just as our soul prospers; to give us and our children increase over and over. His plans are not to harm us and to give us a life of abundance—things filled with hope, love, joy, and peace (Psalm 115:14; 3 John 1:2, Jeremiah 29:11, Romans 15:3).

I laid down emotional wounds from childhood and scars of what I witnessed and experienced that affected how I love myself and respond to others. I surrendered the need for my mom to nurture me and not sacrifice my needs over her self-sufficiency. Prioritization was a strong desire in my marriage. Not being a priority was upsetting. Unbeknownst to myself, neither was I prioritizing my needs over others. I laid down the wounds of not coming first over my spouse's friends, family and emotional habits. I laid down everything that made me feel like I was not valuable, that my opinions and suggestions did not matter, and that my thoughts were not good enough. I stand on Matthew 6:33 (ESV), *"But seek first the kingdom of God and his righteousness,…"* I love God, myself and then neighbors. No one will come before God and His Kingdom. He is the head and not the tail. The last shall be first and the first last.

I surrendered to the Word of God and stood on it. I will not be moved by anything other than the Word and influences of God. I stand on 1 Corinthians 15:58 to be steadfast, immovable, always abounding in the work of the Lord, knowing that my labor is not in vain in the Lord.

Surrendering is a personal decision to release control and let go of everything that has negatively affected life and all its attachments. It accepts and receives what Jesus Christ did on the cross and everything it stood for. When the burden is heavy and hard to bear, put it back on the cross (Matthew 11:28-30). Jesus already died in the flesh, so I do not have to live with emotional wounds but for Him (2 Corinthians 5:15). When we live for Him, the treasure we receive is a supply of abundance. The measure in which we surrender is the measure of our faith and trust in God.

Questions:

What can you stand and surrender to? Search the Bible for scriptures to stand on to encourage and strengthen you to triumph on your victory journey.

_____

_____

_____

_____

_____

Read the Word of God to recognize Him. Hear the Words of God to identify His voice. Receive the Word of God for transformation. Speak the Word of God from the heart to activate.

Prayer:

"Then Jesus cried out with a loud voice, 'Father, I surrender my Spirit into your hands.' And he took his last breath and died" (Luke 23:46 TPT).

Thank You, Lord, for not getting off the cross. You loved me so that much You stayed on the cross. Thank You for fulfilling Your assignment and surrendering to God's Will that we may do the same for our purpose and restoration. Amen.

CHAPTER 9

PURPOSE

"Loneliness is the absence of a person or people.
Alone is the absence of purpose."

Abandonment left me alone, feeling empty, insecure and unfulfilled. It was aloneness that set me apart to grow in Christ. I did not see my purpose; I wanted to know why I existed. I was grateful, but not happy with my life. Dissatisfied and focused on the negative by comparing myself to others, I prevented my dreams from coming true.

There was an emotional disconnection, as I could not feel love. I saw joy and excitement through other's successes and empathy through their sadness, but I was mentally distant from emotions of positivity in my mind. I sensed fulfillment in helping others, serving in the community and worshiping the Lord.

Although I had material things, people in my life and accomplishments, something vital was missing, but did not know where. I felt unfulfilled when I did not have everything I wanted. Growing up in my adolescent stage, I thought being married was the satisfaction that every woman needed to be complete with an excellent education and a successful career. I did not know there was more to life.

I tried to combat my emotions with physical attachments and companionship. I lusted after the things of the eye rather than desiring things of the Spirit—overspending and overeating to compensate for the emotional flux. I lacked full connection and did not get what I wanted. I tried to convince myself that I had what I needed to be satisfied, but I was only kidding myself.

The imperativeness of parents knowing and cultivating their children's purpose in their youth will help them facilitate the concept and monitor their actions for their growth and development. Without preparation and knowledge of purpose, people perish. I was lost for many years because I did not understand my purpose. In my parenting, my focus was knowing God and understanding the scriptures, along with talent and education to have a promising future. I desired to know and understand my purpose for years, but the challenges and personal desires took precedence. It was not until my children were adults that I understood my challenges led me to purpose. Miserably, 52 percent of Americans are blocked and not living in the present because no one commissioned or prepared them to live and understand their purpose from childhood.[7]

Amid the void, I found myself and discovered that I was neglecting my life and was not walking in truth. I was treating myself the way I did not want to live. Yet, I was never alone. God is forever present; everyone I needed was near and with me.

Self-sabotage, thinking I was not good enough, placed limits on my ability to have more. I blocked my blessing by setting aside personal projects or procrastinating, abandoning dreams and goals. I thought all I had was all I got; if I did not see it, it did not exist. I set limits on God.

When I refused to show up for others without showing up for myself first, I noticed that showing up for myself was not satisfying and lacked fulfillment. Being competitive and chasing after success was also tiring. Working on crafts, accomplishing goals, receiving awards and recognition, involving our children in activities, and connecting with peers and church members did not satisfy me. I checked community involvement, goals and accomplishments off my bucket list. I wondered how a pattern of successes (with difficulties) did not have a fulfilled connection to anything that I accomplished. I felt discontent because my yearning belonged to my spirit, not my body or this world.

Christ came so that I might have life and life abundantly, but my actions did not fulfill me. I was doing the things I desired and thought were reasonable and necessary to succeed, but my goods were of my will and not the Will of the Father. I sought success in thinking of myself but not in the beneficial way for my purpose. My achievements are accomplishments but not fulfillments if not used for fulfilling His purpose.

"A thief is only there to steal and kill and destroy. I came so they can have real and eternal life, more and better life than they ever dreamed of" (John 10:10 MSG).

"The thief's purpose is to steal and kill and destroy. My purpose is to give them a rich and satisfying life" (John 10:10 NLT).

I learned that success is not outstanding success unless there is the Word of God, and there is no fulfillment in the void unless it is with the Word of God and a relationship with Him. Being surrounded by loved ones does not move me like the company of the Holy Spirit. When I invite the Holy Spirit to accompany me with the people, I am fulfilled and joyful in the company of others. When I have my rhythm and flow there, He is with me and my mind stays with Him.

Matthew 6:33 tells all to seek the Kingdom of God and His righteousness first. God's masterpiece is inside us. Luke 17:20 lets the believers know that the Kingdom of God is within us. If so, the Kingdom of God is to seek out the mystery inside us and not what is outside of us.

Separating ourselves from society for purpose development and knowing who we are gives us the ability to learn and grow. It allows us to be in the right standing, with uprightness, to do good and not evil, to walk in love. In Jeremiah 1:5 (NLT), God said, *"I knew you before I formed you in your mother's womb. Before you were born, I set you apart and appointed you…"* God's Word reassured me that something unique and essential in my life was more important than just having a spouse and companionship nearby to share it with.

I came into the knowledge of our existence in God. The Father, the Son and the Holy Spirit are all one spirit—the trinity. Our creation in their image and likeness is the spirit of being. God predestined us for adoption to Himself as sons [daughters] through

Jesus Christ, according to the purpose of His Will (Ephesians 1:5).

I had to forgive and let go of anyone who walked away. God is making room for more development within me every time someone departs, turns and walks away—all necessary for growth, development and improvement. Mindfulness of making purposeful decisions and asking the Holy Spirit for guidance into the next phase is assurance in Christ.

We must not chase answers from people for validation. We must plan and ask the Lord to lead us into our next. When we live in the Spirit and aim to please God, we do not look to fulfill the desires of the flesh. The Spirit of God directs and leads all our ways. *"And whatever you do, whether in word or deed, do it all in the name of the Lord Jesus, giving thanks to God the Father through him"* (Colossians 3:17 NIV). Comfort is not in our service to people, but in the service to God. God called man to fulfill His purpose. Service to people is necessary to walk with purpose. All things work together for the good of those called according to His purpose for their life.

Confession of the Heart

- ❖ I am not who the world says I am; I am who God says I am.
- ❖ I am not the result of my situation or my circumstance. I am not my problem.
- ❖ I was not born to live in loneliness, but on purpose. The effects of my past do not recognize me.
- ❖ I know my place, position and purpose. God set me apart and anointed me to serve in a time like this.

CHAPTER 10

LOVING SELF

*"You cannot escape the
consequences of one's actions."*

*"But I this I say: He who sows sparingly will also
reap sparingly, and he who sows bountifully will
also reap bountifully"* (2 Corinthians 9:6 NKJV).

During our marriage, my husband and I had our
family, a home, celebrations, a church home, and
needs. We were big givers. We had some of the most
romantic surprises. Despite that, an element of love
was missing. We both grew up in loving households
with challenges, and our families extended love to
each other. For anyone looking from the outside, the
expression and sharing of love were present, but I was
stuck on not knowing love. I felt out of touch with
love.

During my first military deployment, I read a book
that encouraged reciting "I love you" in the mirror.
As awkward as it was to say, "I love you" to myself, I
learned how much I genuinely cared for myself—not

much. It was disheartening that I could not express love for myself. The love I expected to reciprocate, I could not fathom to have for myself. The Word of the Lord said, *"And the second, like it, is this: 'You shall love your neighbor as yourself.' There is no other commandment greater than these."* (Mark 12:31 NKJV). According to Merriam-Webster, the neighbor is "one living or located near another; (adj) being immediately adjoining or relatively nearby." Therefore, a neighbor is anyone I encounter.

How can one desire love and not know what it means to love oneself? So, I engaged in topics and reflected on love and the compositions of love. There was a more profound revelation of love I yearned for, aside from what I received and gave.

Before our third time apart, I realized I did not know how to relate or respond to love. I could return and extend love, but receiving love and kindness from others was a challenge. I guarded my heart. If someone was not a close relative or friend, it was hard to reciprocate, or perhaps it was not genuine. But I wanted to know about authentic love. So, I had the most incredible love experience at a women's retreat in the mountains. I experienced nothing like it and it was truly divine.

I recall a day in the season of my giving when, in prayer, the Lord said, "Only give out of excess." I responded, "Yes, Lord," and put it on my vision board as a reminder to not sacrifice giving from what I was trying to build financially. I was giving out of my lack and not my excess regarding love and the Lord knew it. I asked nothing further and I perceived that the Holy Spirit referred to my monetary giving. But giving is more than financial when it comes to love. If I am not loving myself and not delighting in time with God for myself, what love do I have to share?

I started with a desire to learn about love for years. I studied love because I felt I did not know who I was without my spouse until I drew closer to Jesus. I also realized that I was trying to attach myself to my spouse to fill the void of love, not loneliness. We loved each other, but I did not have love for myself; I feared managing life without him. I had to become self-sufficient and reliant on God and use what He equipped me with to fulfill my assignment for His Kingdom.

In the beginning of creation, God gave Adam his assignment before companionship and friendship. Adam labored and reigned over the air, sea and ground before He gave him a woman, his helpmate for companionship. The Bible did not mention any other human beings in the beginning before Eve birthed Cain and Abel. The word 'alone' was first mentioned when God said man should not be alone. Beforehand, Adam was content fulfilling his assignment because there was plenty to do and he had a love relationship with God and through his work for God.

> *"And whatever you do, do it heartily, as to the Lord and not to men,"* (Colossians 3:23 NKJV).

Love is a continuous expression of the heart and not something to make someone feel pleasant for a moment; that is joy. Joy is the gladness and laughter of the Spirit. Love is sharing God's heart and one's love with others, unconditionally.

Love is an internal expression of the heart that forms an outward act towards God, self and others. I had to internalize and learn how to respond to love from God. I learned to love myself through the process and did things that honored me the way God does. Loving me is giving grace to accept that I am a working process and still being shaped, molded and led by the Spirit of God so that I do not lust against the Spirit of God in my flesh.

"Love is patient, love is kind. It does not envy, it does not boast, it is not proud. It does not dishonor others, it is not self-seeking, it is not easily angered, it keeps no record of wrongs. It always protects, always trusts, always hopes, always perseveres. Love does not delight in evil but rejoices with the truth" (1 Corinthians 13:4-7 NIV).

A Void in Time

Loneliness and rejection have similarities involving a lack of belonging, whereas loneliness is a prolonged, negatively expressed sense of social exclusion.[8] Time is a form of space. Quality time was my response to love; thus, the rejection of time left me feeling abandoned. With nothing to fill the void, the rejection of time left me alone. It was a thought I created, agreed with and acted upon. Faced with this emptiness, I coped through prayer and embracing communion with God. I found fulfillment in fellowship, supporting community needs and services, developing my skills, focusing on my goals and plans, completing unfinished projects, planning for retirement and family celebrations, and dedicating time to developing skills. It's vital to embrace the power of quality time because it's the key to a joyful and meaningful existence.

Life and marriage are not merely for satisfying lustful desires; they are meant to extend God Himself as love. He created us in His likeness. Understanding love comes from the knowledge and experience gained through a relationship with God, the Father, His Son Christ, our Lord and Savior, and the Holy Spirit. This relationship helps us know who He is and who we are through the Spirit of the One who created us.

To truly understand love is to know Christ and the Spirit of God. Love is not just something we receive; it is the essence from which men and women stem. Love is a lifestyle, an expression of the heart and an extension of God's own heart.

Even when we are apart from loved ones for a time, our hearts can continue to grow because God is filling them. However, if the heart is weak and not growing, it may be lacking God's love. Therefore, it is important to strengthen our love in Him before trying to establish love with another person to experience true fulfillment.

We must love ourselves enough to become all that we desire in love and to influence others to create a legacy of love that we have become. The first step of maximizing one's love of oneself is maximizing one's love and time with God, the Father, enough to create a life of intimacy with Him. We cannot become nor influence others with the love we have until we first experience love with the Father. Overcoming a defeated love life is knowing how to give, honor and express love to ourselves through having intimate love experiences with God and His Son, our brother in Heaven and in us.

> *"…but the greatest of these is love"*
> (1 Corinthians 13:13 NKJV).

CHAPTER 11

MADE WHOLE

"God's the one who rebuilds Jerusalem, who regathers Israel's scattered exiles. He heals the heartbroken and bandages their wounds. He counts the stars and assigns each a name. Our Lord is great, with limitless strength; we'll never comprehend what he knows and does. God puts the fallen on their feet again and pushes the wicked into the ditch" (Psalm 147:2-6 MSG).

We are saved, delivered and set free by our faith in Jesus Christ and God who has given us everything we need. A good example is the biblical story about a disabled man who was waiting for someone to help him.

"In these lay a great multitude of impotent folk, of blind, halt, withered, waiting for the moving of the water. For an angel went down at a certain season into the pool, and troubled the water: whosoever then first after the troubling of the water stepped in was made whole of whatsoever disease he had. And

a certain man was there, which had an infirmity thirty and eight years. When Jesus saw him lie, and knew that he had been now a long time in that case, he saith unto him, Wilt thou be made whole? The impotent man answered him, Sir, I have no man, when the water is troubled, to put me into the pool: but while I am coming, another steppeth down before me. Jesus saith unto him, Rise, take up thy bed, and walk. And immediately the man was made whole, and took up his bed, and walked..."
(John 5:3-9).

That disabled man spent years thinking he needed the help of another man when all he needed was to believe Jesus Christ and obey His command. Jesus is everything he needed back then and He is everything we need today. When I was in a hidden place, I knew my support stood close at hand, ready and eager to assist. I knew what I had in the physical. When my spirit man cried out to Jesus, the Lord rescued me from things I was going through emotionally, but I was still struggling with ups and downs.

I recall the many times I prayed to the Lord to make me whole. Another time, I prayed, thinking about my health; another time, thinking about my relationship; another time, thinking about my mind. I desired wellness in all areas of my life. I want to be whole. I thought about the woman with the issue of blood in the Bible. She thought, 'if I could touch the hem of His garment, I would be made whole' (Matthew 9:21). She made her way through the noise in her thoughts and overcame the fear of what society thought about her. She was at a point where she did not worry about how people would condemn her; she just wanted to be made well within.

For 12 years, the lady was dealing with an issue of blood—and blood runs deep. I believe blood was a figurative term used to describe the blood that runs through our veins, genetically, and the blood of Jesus. I think that after 12 years, she had enough of her issues because the issues affected her physically, relationally, intellectually, and spiritually. She knew she would have wholeness if she could connect spiritually with Jesus.

Everyone must move beyond the crowd and connect with the Lord—just be one with the Savior to feel complete in life. For the woman with issue of blood who wanted to be made whole, the virtue of Jesus transferred to her. He healed her physical pain, her heart to heal her relationally, her mind to heal her mentally, her soul to heal emotionally, and her spirit to heal her faith. Jesus worked on her piece-by-piece until she experienced completeness.

> *"Now may the God of peace Himself sanctify you completely; and may your whole spirit, soul, and body be preserved blameless at the coming of our Lord Jesus Christ"* (1 Thessalonians 5:23 NKJV).

Like the woman with the blood issue, God dealt with me in parts for wholeness. I recall the scripture from Romans 12:4 (AMP): *"For just as in one [physical] body we have many parts, and these parts do not all have the same function or special use."* Within the physical body, God created us in parts: body, soul and spirit. Each part has a different function. The body is the outer shell or vessel and connects with tangible things. The body houses the soul and spirit (1 Corinthians 6:19). The function of the soul is the operation of one's mind, thoughts, emotions, and feelings. The spirit is an element of God that gives life (Galatians 5:16). God said, "Let us make man [and woman] in Our image" (Genesis 1:27).

The image of God is spirit (John 4:24) and the spirit of a man is the lamp of the Lord, which is the consciousness of God's character. The spirit of a man is the lamp of the Lord (Proverbs 20:27). Each part needs love and attention, nourishment to maintain health and strength, and protection from harm and injury to function. *"Guard your heart above all else, for it determines the course of your life"* (Proverbs 4:23 NLT).

One day, in my quiet time with the Lord, He told me to repeat this affirmation thrice daily:

My mind is healed.
My body is healed.
My soul is healed.
My spirit is healed.

Unbeknownst to me, I wondered why I needed to repeat the affirmation, but I recited it daily out of obedience and desire to be made whole. My mind, body, soul, and spirit are now healed, which is a consistent process. Over a period, the more I recited the affirmation, God revealed specific things relating to my mind, body, soul, and spirit that needed healing. Also, things I did not recognize and failed to notice about myself, others and life. I realized He was sharing in parts, not just for me but for the whole world. What He revealed in part was necessary for mending the broken pieces in my mind, body, soul, and spirit.

Thereafter, I started hearing messages and seeing books on healing in particular areas that helped me gain knowledge. The more I cited the affirmation, the

Spirit of the Lord revealed things to me and my understanding increased. For it is written, *"Beloved, I wish above all things that thou mayest prosper and be in health, even as thy soul prospereth"* (3 John 1:2). Healing must be desired from everything that caused hurt and pain to be in good health. The Lord's Will for our lives is to prosper and give us a life of abundance.

> *"But He was wounded for our transgressions, He was crushed for our wickedness [our sin, our injustice, our wrongdoing]; The punishment [required] for our well-being fell on Him, And by His stripes (wounds) we are healed"*
> (Isaiah 53:5 AMP).

Chapter 12

Complete Restoration

*"The work of restorations can begin
once a problem is fully faced."*
– Dana Alexander

I would like to conclude that anyone facing a significant problem may have one or more barriers holding them back and preventing a full recovery. These barriers, or "stones," can dampen a person's spirit, leaving them feeling lifeless. Removing these stones can restore vibrancy and momentum in their life. These stones could symbolize unforgiveness, loneliness, rejection, shame, and depression, which could be stemming from separation, loss or grief. If these stones are not removed, they can grow and create walls of limitation that hinder progress and stifle purpose. Most stones can be removed by shifting the mindset.

In John 4 at the burial location of Lazarus, Jesus demonstrated the process to remove the stone and restore life. When Jesus arrived at the cave where

Lazarus lay dead for four days, He stood before the cave where the stone lay. Then Jesus said, "Remove the stone." Martha, the sister of the deceased, said to Him, "Lord, by this time, there will be a stench, for he has been dead for four days." Jesus addressed Martha's doubt and gave thanks to the Father in Heaven, then cried out in a loud voice, "Lazarus, come out." Lazarus, who had died, emerged, bound hand and foot with wrappings, his face also wrapped in a cloth. Then Jesus said to them, "Loose him and let him go."

Martha represented the voice of negative thoughts and emotional reactions. Jesus did not entertain the negative thoughts or emotions because He understood the power within Him. Lazarus was dormant long enough, the Word came to deal with the root of the problem. Once the stone was displaced, Jesus instructed those with them to help. The burial rags represent every act, decision and entanglement that keeps a person in bondage. The help represented the resources and process to remove the restrictions and for complete restoration.

When Martha went to Jesus, He commanded to remove the stone and instructed the help to remove the rags and grave clothing. When the man lay at the pool, Jesus told him to rise, take up thy bed and walk.

When the woman who desired healing sought Jesus and believed if she touched the hem of His garments, she would be healed, she reached out to Jesus by faith and received healing.

Whatever our reason for waiting, we must let it be for the Lord. We are just prolonging our wait and delaying our promise if the wait is for man. Do not prolong the wait; seek the Lord and His Word, which are found in the Holy Scriptures and prayer. All we need is faith in the size of a mustard seed and movement. If we believe, we can speak authoritatively to any dead thing and reproduce life to our situation, circumstance and purpose. The same resurrection power that raised Jesus from the dead also lives within the believer. Believe there is resurrection and restoration from every dead point in life through the power that works in us according to our faith. In the valley of the dry bones where the sons of God laid slain, the Lord God said to the prophet, *"Speak a prophetic message to the winds, son of man. Speak a prophetic message and say, 'This is what the Sovereign Lord says: Come, O breath, from the four winds! Breathe into these dead bodies so they may live again'"* (Ezekiel 37:9 NLT). And when the prophet did as the Lord God said, breathe returned to the perished.

There is no dead point in life that God cannot save us from. There is no trap the Lord cannot rescue us out of. Do not write your future, hope and purpose off. "Rise up and live." For it is written in John 1:1-5 (NLT), *"In the beginning the Word already existed. The Word was with God, and the Word was God. He* (Jesus) *existed in the beginning with God. God created everything through him* (Jesus), *and nothing was created except through him. The Word gave life to everything created, and his* (Jesus') *life brought light to everyone. The light shines in the darkness, and the darkness can never extinguish it."*

God has called those not moving to excel from displacement, bondage, stagnation, and dormancy. He called us to step out in faith and remove the grave rags that bound us. People seek many things to establish themselves in this world, hindered by pride and lust. Establishments in careers and the marketplace are the places calling for purposes. Voids of purpose are open gaps where stones lay. Living from a purposeful perspective shifts the mindset and helps overcome obstacles and allows us to use those stones to pave paths to our destiny, not one's dismissal.

When I was married, I lived to satisfy a man. Without God, life was not functioning as desired. It was not the boundary that God desired for me.

Setting us apart was one of the best things that happened to me to gain the essential elements for a time like this. Set apart and alone with God is a time of washing, stripping, cleansing, and renewing. Christ built up my spirit. I became in touch with myself and my destiny. God sustained me and I persevered. Out of loneliness, birthed faith and a closer walk with God, dreams, visions of destiny, and fulfillment. I did not lose but gained because I reached up to the Lord. That may not have happened had I not learned the importance of supping with God and building up my spiritual man over my fleshly desire.

> *"He makes me lie down in green pastures; He leads me beside the still waters. He restores my soul; He leads me on paths of righteousness For His name's sake"* (Psalm 23:2-3 NKJV).

All must be dependently and self-sufficiently dependent on God, leaning on His wisdom and resources for the path of life. All eyes [mind and heart] look up to the Lord God, Jehovah. Direct attention and emotions to the Lord. Let the cries of our heart be to Him. This battle is not about anyone but the One who came to save and restore us to Him. Keep pressing toward the mark of our High Calling. In Christ Jesus, the future desired can be obtained.

"You will show me the path of life; In Your presence is fullness of joy; At Your right hand are pleasures forevermore" (Psalm 16:11 NKJV).

CHAPTER 13

PRAYERS AND AFFIRMATIONS

Prayer of Salvation

Romans 10:13; John 3:16, Ephesians 2:8, Romans 10:9

Lord, You will save everyone who calls on Your name. I am a sinner and desire in my heart to be saved. I believe that if I confess with my mouth that Jesus is Lord and believe that You raised Him from the dead, I am saved. Through faith, I received Your saving grace. It is not my doing but Yours. For You so loved the world that You gave Your only Son, that whoever believes in Him should not perish but have eternal life. Thank you for saving me. In Jesus' Name, Amen.

❖ I am free because Christ freed me.
❖ I put off my old self. I am made new.

Prayer of Forgiveness

Psalm 91:16. Matthew 5:25, 1 Corinthians 6:1

Father, I forgive myself and I forgive ____. Please forgive me for the wrong I have done toward You, myself and others. If I confess my sins, You are faithful and will forgive me and cleanse me from all unrighteousness. You will reward me with a long life and give me salvation. If I wronged or angered anyone, I agree with the accuser; I make amends if there are any grievances against another person with me and with them. Give me a heart of reconciliation and help me reconcile any differences I may have with a brother, sister or neighbor. I forgive them and pray they forgive me. In Jesus' Name, Amen.

❖ I decree and declare that God's grace is sufficient in every area of my life.
❖ I am forgiven of all my sins.

Prayer of Repentance

Psalm 54:1, Psalm 51

Have mercy on me, O God, according to Your unfailing love. Because of Your great compassion, blot out the stain of my sins. Wash me clean from my guilt. Purify me from my sin. Vindicate me and deliver my soul. For I recognize my rebellion; it haunts me day and night. I have sinned against You and You alone. I have done what is evil in Your sight. Purify me from my sins and I will be clean. Wash me and I will be whiter than snow. Restore the joy of Your salvation, let me rejoice. And grant me a willing spirit to sustain me. In Jesus' Name, Amen.

❖ I am vindicated and the enemy has no charge over me.
❖ I am renewed. I am a new being.

Prayer of Faith

Mark 11:24, 2 Corinthians 10:5

Lord, thank You for the power You have given me to control my thoughts, bind sad and lonely thoughts, and release every negative and drowning mood. With mustard seed faith, I can move mountains that are blocking me from evolving. With You, Lord, I can do all things. I am no longer intimidated and paranoid about the thoughts I think people have of me. The Holy Spirit, not emotional triggers, leads my renewed mind. I cast down every imagination that says I am lonely. I am not alone, for I know You, Lord, are with me everywhere I go. My mind remains at peace, for the Holy Spirit guides me. I am set apart. In the night's stillness, Father, speak to my heart, fill me with Your love, and remind me of Your goodness and the plans You have for me. In Jesus' Name, Amen.

- ❖ I can do all things through Christ who strengthens me.
- ❖ I am more than a conqueror; I overcome with great joy.

Prayer of Healing

Psalm 25:18; 42:11; 119:25; 119:50, Isaiah 57:19, John 14:27; Romans 8:11

I hope in God, for I will praise You, my Savior and God. Lord, feel my pain and see my trouble. Forgive all my sins. Remove the stone from my heart. My soul clings to the dust; Lord, revive me according to Your Word. The Spirit of God, who raised Jesus from the dead, lives in me. Lord, Jehovah, I am not exempt from Your power. It is Your power that gives life to my mortal body for the same Spirit living within me. I create the fruit of the lips: Peace and joy to Him that is far off and to Him that is near, I receive my healing. Thank You for leaving and giving me peace. In Jesus' Name, Amen.

❖ I am healed and I am whole. I will not be troubled.
❖ Peace surrounds me. Everywhere I am, I share peace.

Prayer of Fulfillment

Romans 12:1-2; Zechariah 9:12;
2 Corinthians 9:8

Lord, help me pull away from what was, when it was, and how it was to what is now that I may enjoy the blessing in my life today and tomorrow. Refresh and renew my spirit according to Your Word and Scripture. Renew and transform my heart and mind to Your kindness, compassion, love, forgiveness, and understanding that I will be able to do what is of the good and acceptable Will of God. Help me to steward Your love in the family so that all will be lifted. In Jesus' Name, Amen.

❖ The love and presence of the Lord fills me.
❖ I am prosperous in God's plan for me.
❖ The blessing of the overflow overwhelms me with great and mighty things of God.
❖ I am a prisoner of hope. The Lord will restore twice as much to me.

<u>Prayer of the Heart</u>

Ephesians 1:12; 1 Peter 5:10; Philippians 2:2

Great Jehovah, thank You that Your hope does not disappoint. Fill the empty spaces of my heart and any family and friend who is dealing with void and emptiness in the heart. Refill, refuel and energize our heart. Pour Your love upon us. May Your love consume and Your peace comfort. May Your love and joy flow like a river that never runs dry in our lives. Refresh us with Your presence. Let Your amazing wonders overtake us. May there be continuous peace and sweet communion and comfort in Jesus' Name. Amen.

- ❖ I love God and I am me.
- ❖ I lack no good thing; God fills the void.
- ❖ I am healed and I am whole.

Prayer for the Reader

Father, touch every individual who reads this book and partook of the outpour of my heart. Bless them with the goodness that only flows from Your love. Bless them as they strive to renew their understanding of life and positions here on the earth. Speak to their heart consistently. Lead, guide and direct their heart and mind in the way it should go. Have mercy and show them Your face, Your love, Your hand, and Your faithfulness. May the doors of their heart remain open to You and closed to stagnating emotions. Deliver them from all unrighteousness. Heal and lift them up from painful experiences and circumstances of past hurt, wounds and trauma. Teach and show them Your way. Guide their steps and emotions out of the old and adorn themselves with the splendor of Your glory. May they endeavor to walk in humility, remain prayerful and discover boldness and strength in You. May the mysteries of Your love keep them in awe of You. This I cover in Jesus' Name. Amen.

Forever in Your Love,
Dana ~ Your Daughter

"May He grant you out of the riches of His glory, to be strengthened and spiritually energized with power through His Spirit in your inner self, [indwelling your innermost being and personality]," (Ephesians 3:16 AMP).

ABOUT THE AUTHOR

Dr. Dana Johnson is an author, speaker, mentor, minister, Army retired veteran, and founder of InspireHer to Rise, LLC. Her approach to helping the abandoned, rejected and lonely uses her RISE UP application from revelations, biblical principles and personal experience. She is a voice among Christ-filled women speakers and leaders with the Vessels of Honor, Women of Movement and Christian Speaker Foundation. Dr. Johnson was a guest on PromoteHer with Titus Two Talk and Podcasting Guests. She shares inspiring words on YouTube and social media platforms.

Website: www.drdanaj.com

RESOURCES

[1] A National Survey of Adults 45 and Older Loneliness and Social Connections. Retrieved from AARP doi.org/10.26419/res.00246.001

[2] Goddard, I. & Parker, K. (2025, January). Men, Women and Social Connections. Pew Research Center. Retrieved from https://pewrsr.ch/429NR2i

[3] Barreto, M., Victor, C., Hammond, C., Eccles, A., Richins, M. T., & Qualter, P. (2021). Loneliness around the world: Age, gender, and cultural differences in loneliness. Personality and individual differences, 169, 110066.

[4] Cené CW, Beckie TM, Sims M, et al. (2022). Effects of Objective and Perceived Social Isolation on Cardiovascular and Brain Health: A Scientific Statement from the American Heart Association. Journal of the American Heart Association. 2022;11(16):e026493

[5] Sakai, K. (2023, February). How loneliness reshapes the brain. (2024). Neuroscience. Retrieved from https://www.quantamagazine.org/how-loneliness-reshapes-the-brain-20230228/

[6] Trotta, A. (2023, April). How to a handle paranoid thoughts. Retrieved from https://psyche.co/guides/how-to-handle-paranoid-thoughts-by-recognising-false-alarms

[7] Zauderer, S. (2023, July). 49 Loneliness statistics: How many people are lonely?" Cross River Therapy. Retrieved from www.crossrivertherapy.com/research/loneliness-statistics

[8] Stillman TF, B. R. (2009, July). Alone and Without Purpose: Life Loses Meaning Following Social Exclusion. Retrieved from doi: 10.1016/j.jesp.2009.03.007

www.ingramcontent.com/pod-product-compliance
Lightning Source LLC
Chambersburg PA
CBHW071015120626
46546CB00003B/1100